MOUNTAIN LIONS

BIG CATS

BY CHRISTINE ZUCHORA-WALSKE

Consultant: Christina Simmons
San Diego Zoo Global
San Diego, California

CAPSTONE PRESS
a capstone imprint

Edge Books are published by Capstone Press,
1710 Roe Crest Drive, North Mankato, Minnesota 56003.
www.capstonepub.com

Books published by Capstone Press are manufactured with paper
containing at least 10 percent post-consumer waste.

Library of Congress Cataloging-in-Publication Data
Zuchora-Walske, Christine.
  Mountain lions / by Christine Zuchora-Walske.
    p. cm. — (Edge books. Big cats)
  Includes bibliographical references and index.
  ISBN 978-1-4296-7644-1 (library binding : alk. paper)
  1. Puma—Juvenile literature. I. Title.
  QL737.C23Z78 2012
  599.75'24—dc23   2011021017

Summary: "Describes the history, physical features, and habitat of mountain lions"
—Provided by publisher.

Editorial Credits
Brenda Haugen, editor; Kyle Grenz, designer; Svetlana Zhurkin,
    media researcher; Laura Manthe, production specialist

Photo Credits
Alamy: FLPA, 18–19, Papilio, 15; Creatas, 4; Digital Vision, 14; Dreamstime:
Andrew Chin, 21, Chris Lorenz, 24, Pod666, cover, Rinus Baak, 10, 29, Tatagatta,
26, Twildlife, 22, 23, 25; EyeWire, 11; iStockphoto: Denis Jr. Tangney, 28, John
Pitcher, 8; National Geographic Stock: Jim and Jamie Dutcher, 17, Norbert
Rosing, 19 (top); Shutterstock: creative, 27, Dennis Donohue, 1, 7, ecliptic blue,
9, Ronnie Howard, 6, S.R. Maglione, 12, 16, Stanislav Eduardovich Petrov
(background), throughout, Tony Rix, 13, 20, visceralimage, 5

Printed in the United States of America in Stevens Point, Wisconsin.
102011   006404WZS12

TABLE OF CONTENTS

CAT OF MANY NAMES

Thousands of years ago, a girl stepped onto the rocky western coast of a strange land. She had come from Asia to the Americas with her people. They were seeking animals to hunt for food and fur. As the people came ashore, the girl spotted a streak of brown fur vanishing into the forest.

Big Cat Fact

Today the mountain lion is known by more than 150 names. It has more names than any other animal in the world.

American Indian
Names for Mountain Lions

Name	Meaning
klandagi	lord of the forest
katalgar	greatest of wild hunters
ko-icto	cat of god
puma	mighty magic animal

European
Names for Mountain Lions

Name	Meaning
leon	lion
leopardo	leopard
tyger	tiger
catamount	cat of the mountain

Four hundred years ago, a boy splashed onto the eastern coast of the same land. He had come from Europe to the Americas with his family. They were hoping to start a better life. As he helped unload supplies, the boy felt eyes upon him. He scanned the swampy shoreline. He saw a big cat just as it slipped into the trees.

Mountain lions once prowled all over North and South America. They lived from coast to coast and from Canada to Chile. Many people saw the big cats. These people lived in different times and places, and they spoke different languages. So they gave the mountain lion dozens of different names.

5

Chapter 1

MOUNTAIN LIONS TODAY

Modern scientists call the mountain lion *Puma concolor*, which means "puma of one color." Most people call this big cat a mountain lion, cougar, or puma.

The mountain lion no longer lives all over North and South America. As people spread across the continents, they crowded mountain lions out of some areas.

The mountain lion still has a big **range**, though. Today mountain lions live in Central America and western North America. They also can be found in most of South America.

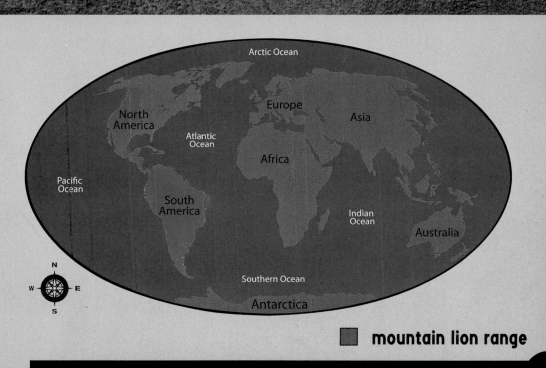

mountain lion range

NO MOUNTAINS REQUIRED

Mountain lions don't always live in the mountains. They can live anywhere that has plenty of **prey**. Deer are one of the mountain lion's most common prey. Mountain lions often live in brushy or wooded areas crowded with deer.

prey—an animal hunted by another animal for food

Big Cat Fact

Hunting can be dangerous for mountain lions. They often hunt prey that is larger than they are. Sometimes large prey injures or kills attacking mountain lions.

Mountain lions also need plenty of **cover** to hide them. Cover can be trees, underbrush, boulders, or rock ledges. Mountain lions use cover to sneak up on prey. Mountain lions also need cover for resting and for raising their young.

WHAT'S THE DIFFERENCE?

A mountain lion resembles other big cats. It's similar in size and shape to the leopard and the jaguar. It shares some of its range with jaguars.

But mountain lions are still unique. They are smaller than tigers and lions. Unlike tigers, leopards, jaguars, and cheetahs, mountain lions have no distinct markings. And while many other big cats can roar, mountain lions can't.

ONE BIG CAT

A mountain lion's body is strong and sturdy. Adults stand about 30 inches (76 centimeters) high at the shoulder. They stretch 5 to 8 feet (1.5 to 2.5 meters) from nose to tail tip.

Size Comparison Chart

The average height of an American male is 5 feet, 10 inches (178 cm).

One-third of this length is the big cat's tail. A long tail helps the lion keep its balance. Mountain lions weigh 80 to 180 pounds (36 to 82 kilograms). Most of this weight is muscle. A mountain lion's hind legs are longer than its front legs, which helps the big cat leap.

Big Cat Fact

Mountain lions can leap 45 feet (14 m) over the ground or 15 feet (5 m) into the air.

Chapter 2

HUNTING FOR SURVIVAL

A mule deer rests in a thicket of oak shrubs. It nibbles on the shiny green leaves. Out of sight up the rocky hillside, a mountain lion slowly approaches. Its sleek brown body flows silently from boulder to boulder. Several yards away, the mountain lion stops. It crouches low and holds perfectly still. Every muscle is tensed, ready to spring.

The deer shifts to nibble a new branch. Now it's facing away from the lion. The lion pounces. In one huge leap, it lands at the deer's side. It grabs the deer's shoulders with its claws. It then bites the back of the deer's neck, snapping its spine. The deer drops to the ground and is soon dead.

ON THE PROWL

Mountain lions are **carnivores**. Mountain lions prefer fresh meat, so they must hunt and kill prey. Mountain lions hunt any prey they can catch.

LONE STALKER

A lone adult North American mountain lion kills about one deer every two weeks. A mother lion with a litter of cubs might kill one deer every few days.

Mountain lions are solitary **predators**. They live and hunt alone. They often hunt at dawn and dusk, when deer are most active.

Big Cat Fact

A female mountain lion's territory is usually between 50 and 75 square miles (129 and 194 square kilometers). A male's territory is usually at least 90 square miles (233 sq. km). The size of a mountain lion's territory mainly depends upon how much prey is available.

predator—an animal that hunts other animals for food

To find food, a mountain lion walks its **territory** in zigzags. It tries to stay hidden among rocks and trees. It uses all its senses to detect any sound, smell, or movement.

When a mountain lion discovers prey, it starts stalking the animal. The mountain lion crouches close to the ground and quietly inches closer. It freezes repeatedly to avoid being seen. The mountain lion stretches its head out, spreads its whiskers, and perks up its ears, watching the prey's every move.

THE KILL

When the prey is within 50 feet (15 meters), the mountain lion attacks. It sprints or leaps, landing at the animal's rear or side. A mountain lion's powerful jaw clamps down on its prey like a vise. It seizes the prey's shoulders and neck with its razor-sharp claws to keep the animal from escaping.

Next the mountain lion usually bites its prey on the back of the neck. A mountain lion's strong jaws and sharp teeth slice through its prey's muscle and spine. The prey dies quickly. It has little chance to fight back and injure the mountain lion.

The mountain lion drags or carries its food to a protected place. If the prey is small, the mountain lion eats it all. If the prey is large, the mountain lion rips open its body behind the ribs. A mountain lion often eats the heart, lungs, and liver first. Then it eats the big muscles of the thighs and shoulders. If the big cat is still hungry, it moves on to the legs.

Leftovers

When a mountain lion is full, it covers up its uneaten prey. It rakes leaves, twigs, dirt, or rocks over the **carcass**. This covering hides and protects the food. A mountain lion's urge to cover its leftovers is so strong that it will place a single twig on top of a carcass if nothing else is available. Then the lion leaves. It may return later and eat more. Or it may abandon the carcass—especially if the meat spoils or another animal finds it.

carcass- the body of a dead animal   19

BLENDING IN

A mountain lion must hunt to survive. Its body is perfectly suited to the hunting life. Plain brown fur helps the lion sneak up on prey. The color blends in with trees, brush, and rocks.

SENSES

A mountain lion has keen senses. These senses help the mountain lion find and attack its food.

The big cat can see well at any time of day or night. Its eyes face forward and work together, helping the mountain lion judge distances correctly.

A mountain lion also has excellent hearing. Its rounded ears hear a wider range of sounds than human ears do. The mountain lion can move its ears separately to pick up different sounds coming from different directions.

The big cat's other senses are also important. Its nose can identify odors in the air or follow a scent trail on the ground.

When a mountain lion attacks, it uses its sense of touch. A mountain lion's whiskers, nose, jaws, and paws are very sensitive. They help the big cat grab and bite in exactly the right place—even in the dark.

Chapter 3

RAISING YOUNG

A female mountain lion walks up a hillside. Her big belly swings beneath her. She stops at a cluster of boulders. A few small trees grow from the crevices, providing shelter from the sun and rain. This will make a good den. She lies down in the shade to rest. It's almost time for her cubs to be born.

Like all **_____**, mountain lion babies drink milk from their mother. Cubs start drinking milk within minutes after birth.

BABIES ON BOARD

Many animals give birth only in the spring. But mountain lions can mate and give birth at any time of year. A female mountain lion has young about once every other year.

A female is pregnant for about three months. She usually gives birth to two or three cubs. Newborn mountain lions are tiny and fluffy. They weigh about 1 pound (0.5 kg). Their ear canals and eyes are closed. Their light brown coats have dark brown spots. This coloring helps the cubs blend in with grass and brush.

mammal—a warm-blooded animal that breathes air and has hair or fur; female mammals feed milk to their young

GROWING UP

When cubs are about 2 weeks old, their eyes and ears open. They begin walking around. They spend most of their time sleeping, eating, and playing. Playing helps cubs learn hunting skills, such as stalking, pouncing, and biting.

Cubs begin eating meat when they are about 2 months old. At first their mother brings chunks of meat to the den. Later she leads her cubs to carcasses. The cubs eat the kill and play with it. Playing with the dead animal is important for mountain lion cubs. It helps the cubs sharpen their hunting skills. At about 3 months, cubs stop drinking milk and eat only meat.

Cubs lose their spots when they are between 3 and 15 months old. At around 6 to 9 months, they begin leaving their mother for short trips. They try hunting on their own. When they are 1 year old, cubs can kill small animals, such as birds and squirrels.

A cub leaves its mother when it is 1 to 2 years old. It then searches for a territory of its own.

ADULTHOOD

A mountain lion becomes an adult at about 2 years old. Once it reaches adulthood, it can mate. Mountain lions find mates mainly by smell. They also use sounds. A female screams to signal that she is looking for a mate. An interested male screams in reply.

Big Cat Fact

A mountain lion's scream may appeal to other mountain lions, but it's terrifying to people. It sounds like a person screaming in fear.

Chapter 4

DANGEROUS LIVES

Adult mountain lions have no natural enemies except for people. Still, their lives are full of danger.

People cause most adult mountain lion deaths. Some people hunt mountain lions for sport. They enjoy the challenge of bringing down a big cat. Other hunters believe that mountain lions kill too many pets and farm animals. These hunters kill the lions to protect dogs, cats, cattle, horses, and sheep. Some mountain lions get run over by cars.

NEXT 10 MILES

Cubs face even greater risk than adult mountain lions. Cubs are small and weak. Many cubs become snacks for other predators. Less than half of mountain lion cubs live to adulthood. Cubs that manage to grow up usually live eight to 10 years.

Big Cat Fact

Researchers have found that some mountain lions live almost 20 years in the wild, but those cases are rare.

NATURAL DEATHS

A small number of mountain lions die young
from natural causes. Disease is rare. Mountain lions
spend most of their time alone and seldom come
in contact with germs or pests. However, some
mountain lions die from fights with prey or other
mountain lions. A few die of natural causes after
reaching an old age.

HUMAN HELPERS

Mountain lions face many threats, especially in areas where lots of people live. But mountain lions are not **endangered**.

Many people are working to prevent the cats from ever becoming endangered. Scientists study the mountain lion's body and behavior. Learning more about mountain lions helps people find better ways to protect the big cats. Some people work to heal injured mountain lions. Others teach people how to share the land safely and peacefully with mountain lions. Efforts to keep mountain lions safe will help make sure these big cats will continue to survive.

GLOSSARY

carcass (KAHR-kuhs)—the body of a dead animal

carnivore (KAHR-nuh-vohr)—an animal that eats only meat

cover (KUH-ver)—an object that hides an animal from other animals

endangered (en-DAYN-juhrd)—at risk of dying out

mammal (MAM-uhl)—a warm-blooded animal that breathes air and has hair or fur; female mammals feed milk to their young

predator (PRED-uh-tur)—an animal that hunts other animals for food

prey (PRAY)—an animal hunted by another animal for food

range (RAYNJ)—a geographic region where an animal or plant species naturally lives

territory (TER-uh-tor-ee)—an area of land that an animal claims as its own to live in

READ MORE

Gagne, Tammy. *Lions.* Big Cats. Mankato, Minn.: Capstone Press, 2012.

Markle, Sandra. *Mountain Lions.* Animal Predators. Minneapolis: Lerner Publishing, 2010.

Raatma, Lucia. *Mountain Lions.* Community Connections: How Do We Live Together? Ann Arbor, Mich.: Cherry Lake Pub., 2010.

INTERNET SITES

FactHound offers a safe, fun way to find Internet sites related to this book. All of the sites on FactHound have been researched by our staff.

Here's all you do:

Visit *www.facthound.com*

Type in this code: 9781429676441

 **Super-cool stuff!** Check out projects, games and lots more at **www.capstonekids.com**

INDEX